RAOUL WALLENBERG

THE HOLOCAUST™

RAOUL WALLENBERG

EMMA SIMON AND
THOMAS STREISSGUTH

ROSEN
PUBLISHING®

Published in 2016 by The Rosen Publishing Group, Inc.
29 East 21st Street, New York, NY 10010

First Edition

Library of Congress Cataloging-in-Publication Data

Simon, Emma, 1980– author.
Raoul Wallenberg/Emma Simon and Thomas Streissguth.—First edition.
pages cm.— (The Holocaust)
Includes index.
ISBN 978-1-4994-6242-5 (library bound)
1. Wallenberg, Raoul, 1912-1947—Juvenile literature. 2. Righteous Gentiles in the Holocaust—Biography—Juvenile literature. 3. Diplomats—Sweden—Biography—Juvenile literature. 4. World War, 1939–1945—Jews—Rescue—Hungary—Juvenile literature. 5. Holocaust, Jewish (1939–1945)—Hungary—Juvenile literature. 6. Hungary—Ethnic relations—Juvenile literature. I. Streissguth, Thomas, 1958– author. II. Title.
D804.66.W35S55 2016
940.53'18092—dc23
[B]

2015025143

Manufactured in China

CONTENTS

INTRODUCTION

On March 19, 1944, Germany occupied Hungary during World War II (1939–1945). Hungary's Admiral Miklós Horthy was allowed to remain Regent, and the German government made General Döme Sztójay prime minister. Sztójay was entrusted to carry out—along with Lieutenant Colonel Adolf Eichmann, commander of Germany's *Schutzstaffel* ("Protective Echelon," known as SS, the elite corps of soldiers of the Nazi Party), and his SS officers—the deportation of Hungarian Jews to the concentration camp Auschwitz, in German-occupied Poland, and other Nazi concentration camps. According to the U.S. Holocaust Memorial Museum in Washington, D.C., by July 1944, more than 440,000 Jews from

In 2013, Judith (Kopstein) Weiszmann and her grandsons pose in front of a Canadian postage stamp that commemorates Raoul Wallenberg and the special diplomatic pass for fourteen-year-old Judith that Wallenberg used to save her from being deported by the Nazis in Budapest, Hungary, in 1944.

Hungary had been deported. Nearly 320,000 of these people were killed on their arrival to Auschwitz. Thousands of Hungarian Jews were also transported to the border with Austria, where they would be forced to dig fortification trenches for the Germans.

November 29, 1944, was a busy day at the Josef Varos train station in Budapest, Hungary. Angry guards shoved frightened men toward the open doors of a cattle train. The train's engineer fired his locomotive, sending swirls of black smoke up and down the platform. The shouts of the guards mixed with the sound of gunfire and the barking of dogs. Hearing the dogs and seeing the rifles and machine guns, the men stumbled away from them, into the dark freight cars. Sliding doors closed behind them. Bolts and fasteners moved into place with a loud, heavy clatter. Within a few minutes, hundreds of men were locked in the train. There were eighty men to each car. They stood shoulder to shoulder. There was no food and no place to sit or lie down.

The operation went smoothly. The guards were sending away a trainload of Jewish workers. The workers would travel to Austria. There they would build trenches and other fortifications to help German troops fighting against the armies of the Soviet Union. When the work was finished, the workers would be sent to a concentration camp. There they would be murdered. Standing nearby and closely watching the train were SS officers. Eichmann had arranged for this train. He was determined to murder every last Jew in Hungary. There were few Hungarians willing or able to stop him.

One of the officers saw a man dressed in a civilian coat and hat run along the platform toward him. The man was waving his arms, yelling, and cursing. The officer drew himself up and pulled out his revolver. He placed it just inches from the man's stomach. The civilian grew angrier. He began jumping up and down and screaming. Although he was a Swede, he spoke perfect German. He ordered the officer to stop the operation immediately.

Guards and prisoners watched the strange argument. Nervous and unsure of what to do, the SS officer put his gun away. The man in civilian clothes quickly moved away and walked up and down alongside the train. He barked orders at the men on the platform and at the men aboard the train. He asked for papers—everybody must show their papers. All those with papers must get off the train immediately.

The prisoners searched their pockets. They pulled out passes, certificates, bills, scraps, and any piece of paper with printing on it. The civilian sat down at a table, drawing the men away from the train with his loud, commanding voice. He pulled out blank papers of his own, signed them quickly, and handed them out. He pointed toward a line of trucks waiting outside the station. Three hundred men climbed into the trucks.

The civilian left. He had just tricked the SS officer into sparing the lives of three hundred men. He had first arrived in Budapest on July 9, 1944, and had been doing the same secretive rescue operation for nearly five months in this dangerous and violent place far from his home. His name was Raoul Wallenberg.

CHAPTER ONE

GROWING UP IN SWEDEN AND PREPARING FOR A CAREER

Raoul Gustav Wallenberg was born in Kappsta, on the island of Lidingö, near Stockholm, Sweden, on August 4, 1912. His father, Raoul Oscar Wallenberg, had served as an officer in the Swedish navy. But the elder Raoul Wallenberg died of cancer in May 1912 at the age of twenty-three—just three months before the birth of his son and eight months after his marriage to Maria "Maj" Sofia Wising. Maj's own father died from pneumonia a few months after Raoul was born. Maj was about twenty-one years old at the time.

Everybody in Sweden knew the name of Wallenberg. Members of this wealthy and prominent family had been bankers, business-men, military officers, government ministers, and diplomats. At the time of Raoul Wallenberg's

Gustav Wallenberg (*left*) was the best man at Count Sigvard Bernadotte's wedding. Bernadotte was the grandson of the king of Sweden. Gustav, Raoul's grandfather, a banker, had powerful political and financial connections in Sweden.

birth, his grandfather, Gustav Wallenberg, was Sweden's ambassador to Japan.

CHILDHOOD

In 1918, Maj Wallenberg remarried. Her second husband, Fredrik von Dardel, worked in Sweden's Ministry of Health. He eventually became an administrator of Sweden's Karolinska Hospital, world-renowned for research in medicine. Maj and Fredrik von Dardel had two children, Guy and Nina. They were the younger half brother and half sister of Raoul Wallenberg.

Raoul enjoyed a happy childhood. His mother and stepfather watched over him. His grandfather looked after his education. Raoul attended good schools and had many friends. But with the name Wallenberg also came responsibility. Gustav Wallenberg wanted his grandson to become a businessman or a banker. The Wallenbergs owned the Enskilda Bank and

Gustav expected Raoul to work at this bank. Gustav also had the idea to set up an international Wallenberg bank someday. If Raoul proved himself, he might become the president of this bank.

Buildings interested Raoul much more than money or banking, however. He spent long hours at construction sites, watching the work in progress. He learned everything he could about architecture. He read many books about how buildings were designed and erected.

THE SWEDISH MILITARY AND COLLEGE

After high school, where he excelled in Russian and drawing, Raoul spent nine months in the military. (All Swedish men had to perform military service after they finished school.) Gustav then arranged for Raoul to travel to and live in foreign countries, including France. He knew that many Swedes never traveled, and he wanted something different for his grandson: the experience of foreign cultures and foreign languages.

In 1931, Raoul left for the United States. There he enrolled at the University of Michigan, in the city of Ann Arbor. He studied his favorite subject, architecture. Wallenberg graduated with honors from the university in 1935. He had earned his architecture degree, typically a five-year program, in just three-and-a-half years. For his good academic work, Wallenberg won a school prize.

Wallenberg arrived in Ann Arbor, Michigan, in 1931 to study architecture at the University of Michigan. He graduated in 1935, and when he was unable to work as an architect, his grandfather encouraged him to travel and learn business.

Wallenberg did not live in Ann Arbor the whole time he was in the United States. He traveled all over the western region of the country and toured Mexico. In the summer of 1933, he worked at the Chicago World's Fair, at the Swedish pavilion.

Wallenberg often hitchhiked. He was young and didn't worry much about the dangers of asking for rides from strangers. Once, while returning to Ann Arbor from Chicago, he was picked up by four men in a car. Soon afterward, the men drove off the main road and onto a dirt lane. There they robbed Wallenburg at gunpoint.

Wallenberg was carrying very little money. But instead of panicking, he calmly asked the thieves for a ride back to the highway. They agreed at first. But his coolness made them so nervous they soon changed their minds. They dumped him in a ditch and fled the scene.

The robbers didn't harm him, but they did teach Wallenberg an important lesson. He didn't always need a weapon or physical strength to face an enemy. Sometimes self-confidence and a strong voice were all that he required.

TRAVELING AND LEARNING ABOUT BUSINESS

After returning to Sweden, Wallenberg was unable to find a job as an architect. He would follow the career that his grandfather had prepared for him—

WALLENBERG LEGACY ENDOWMENT

In 1985, some professors and administrators at the University of Michigan founded the Wallenberg Legacy Endowment to honor their esteemed alumnus. Annually, the endowment sponsors a lecture on the Ann Arbor campus and awards the Wallenberg Medal to someone who has displayed moral courage in his or her life. The medal commemorates Wallenberg's bravery and resolve in rescuing Jews from the evil snares of the Nazis. Medal recipients who have presented lectures throughout the years include Elie Wiesel (a Nobel Laureate, humanitarian, and Auschwitz survivor), Jan Karski (a Polish courier who told the Allies about the murder of Jews in Europe), Miep Gies (who hid Anne Frank and her family from the Nazis in Amsterdam), Per Anger (a friend of Wallenberg's who helped to save Jews in Budapest), Marion Pritchard (who protected 150 Dutch Jews, mostly children, during World War II), Simcha Rotem (survivor of the Warsaw Ghetto), Nina Lagergren (Wallenberg's half sister), Bill Basch (a concentration camp survivor who, as a teen, worked as a courier for Wallenberg in Budapest), Heinz Drossel (a German who hid Jews from the Nazis), Aung San Suu Kyi (a Nobel Peace Laureate and advocate of democracy and human rights in Burma), and Agnes Heller (a philosopher and Holocaust survivor), among others.

he would become a serious businessman. Gustav Wallenberg still wanted his grandson to see the world and to meet as many different people as possible. In 1935, he sent Raoul to Cape Town, South Africa. There, he worked as a traveling salesman for the Swedish South African Export/Import Company. He met architects, engineers, and builders. He sold construction materials, and he did well at it. However, Wallenberg earned no money in this job. He was still just a trainee.

After six months, his grandfather arranged another position for Wallenberg, a job in the Holland Bank. The bank had one of its branches in Haifa, a port city in Palestine. Again, Wallenberg worked without pay. In Haifa, he stayed in a boardinghouse where he met Jewish families who had moved to Palestine from Europe. Many of these Jews were fleeing from Germany to escape persecution by the Nazis. In 1933, the Nazi Party had taken power in

Germany. Following the ideas of Adolf Hitler, their leader (Chancellor), the Nazis passed laws to control or harm the Jewish population. Hitler hated

In the 1930s, Adderley Street was a bustling street in the main area of the business district in Cape Town, South Africa. As a salesman trainee, Wallenberg acquired valuable skills involving the import and export business there.

the Jews and blamed them for Germany's defeat in World War I in 1918.

The new laws forced many German Jews to leave their homes and their businesses. Fearing even worse persecution, thousands of Jews fled the country, while others remained behind. Those who remained thought the troubles would pass and that they would survive. They couldn't yet imagine that Hitler and the Nazis were planning to destroy the Jews completely.

WORLD WAR II BEGINS

In Haifa, Wallenberg worked very hard. But he found the banker's life very boring, and he didn't like spending his days handling money. He also didn't like dealing with the bank's many rules and regulations. He hated turning down people who wanted to borrow money. Instead, he wanted to help people, somehow.

In 1937, Gustav Wallenberg died. Without his grandfather's guidance, Raoul felt unsure of what to do. He went into business but failed. He offered designs for buildings and parks in Stockholm, but these projects never left his drawing board. In the fall of 1939, while he was still trying to find his career, Wallenberg heard the news that Germany had invaded Poland. Great Britain and France then declared war on Germany. World War II had begun.

In September 1939, German soldiers cross a bridge during the German invasion of Poland, which marked the beginning of World War II. Sweden remained neutral during the war, but Wallenberg was unable to find employment as an architect.

The war put an end to Wallenberg's plans of becoming an architect. All new construction stopped in Sweden and throughout Europe. The war also prevented Wallenberg from traveling freely, as he once had, on the European continent.

In the spring of 1940, the Nazi armies marched into France, the Netherlands, and Belgium. France surrendered, and German troops marched into Paris, the French capital. Wherever they went, the Nazis began passing new laws against the Jews. They marked Jewish homes and forced Jews to wear yellow stars on their clothing to identify themselves. Members of the SS arrived in German-occupied territory. They arrested, beat, tortured, and murdered Jews wherever they went.

Sweden remained neutral during World War II. The Swedish government did not ally itself with Germany or with Germany's enemies. Because they were neutral, Swedish diplomats could travel anywhere and meet with the leaders of any nation. The Swedes considered their territory, and their people, to be safe from attack and arrest.

After the war began, Wallenberg met Koloman Lauer, a Jewish businessman and refugee. Lauer had left Hungary, his native land, and moved to Sweden. Hungary had allied itself with Nazi Germany, and the Hungarian leaders had passed new anti-Jewish laws of their own. These laws made it impossible for Lauer to stay in Hungary and carry on his business. Lauer's business was the Central European Trading Company. This firm bought and sold food and dry goods in Sweden and the rest of Europe. Because he could no longer travel in much of Europe, Lauer hired Wallenberg as a salesman. Wallenberg's job would be to travel all over the continent for the company.

Wallenberg eagerly accepted the new position. Finally he had found something that suited him well. He loved to travel, and he loved to make deals. He had a gift for languages—he could speak French, German, English, and Russian fluently. He had a knack for sizing up people, for understanding their characters, and for learning what they wanted. He had a friendly, enthusiastic manner and a lot of energy. All these qualities made him an ideal salesman for Koloman Lauer. According to a 1981 tribute posted on the website of the Raoul Wallenberg Committee of the United States, Wallenberg was named a junior partner of the Central European Trading Company within eight months.

CHAPTER TWO

WALLENBERG AND HUNGARY

The Central European Trading Company gave Wallenberg many opportunities for travel internationally. Koloman Lauer dispatched him to such countries as Germany, Switzerland, France, and Romania. Wallenberg first went to Paris, France, in late 1941. By this time, German troops were occupying the city. They strictly controlled people arriving or departing. As a neutral Swede and a businessman, Wallenberg could move around Europe freely. He also traveled to Germany and to Hungary, Lauer's native land. In Budapest, Wallenberg spent several weeks meeting people, doing business, and walking in the streets. He also visited Lauer's family to make sure they were safe.

Hungary had allied itself with Nazi Germany, but it also had one of the largest communities of Jews in Europe. According to a report by the World Jewish Congress, a 1941 census tallied about 846,000 Jews living in Hungary. About 184,000 lived in the Hungarian capital of Budapest. The Jews had been living in Hungary

Posters put up in Paris by the Vichy government, an ally of Nazi Germany, announce a meeting of the National Popular Rally Party in 1941. Wallenberg went to Paris that year and saw firsthand how German troops deported French civilians, including Jews, to work camps.

for more than one thousand years. They made up an important part of Hungarian society. Many of Hungary's lawyers, doctors, merchants, and business owners were Jewish. There were Jewish teachers, artists, writers, and musicians.

Most of the Christian Hungarians accepted the Jewish people who lived among them. Yet Hungary also had an anti-Semitic streak. Some Hungarians saw the Jews as foreigners, even as enemies. In imitation of Germany's Nazi Party, anti-Semites in Hungary formed the Nyilas, or Arrow Cross Party. The Arrow Cross Party had its own uniforms, flags, and symbol—a pair of crossed arrows. But unlike the Nazi Party, the Arrow Cross had won no elections. The leaders of the Arrow Cross had not succeeded in taking power.

While traveling in Europe, Wallenberg had his first experience of life under Nazi occupation. Wherever German armies had

This poster displays the crossed arrow symbol of the Hungarian Arrow Cross Party. The party was founded by Ferenc Szálasi and favored the political philosophy of the Nazi Party of Germany.

conquered, German officers and troops marched confidently through the streets. The Germans wore the swastika, the symbol of Adolf Hitler's Nazi Party, and flew Nazi flags from important government buildings. They set curfews at night, closed down businesses, and arrested people for violating curfew and other rules. German SS troops broke into homes and rounded up Jewish families. They sent their prisoners to concentration camps in the countryside.

In Germany, Wallenberg saw many frightened Jews. Some were still trying to flee the country. But since the start of the war, the Jews had been trapped. They could not leave Germany. They could not even leave their own homes, except for a few hours each day. They were forbidden to run businesses or attend religious services in their synagogues. Their children could not go to school.

These sights deeply affected Wallenberg. He realized that he was doing nothing to help. He felt a strong sympathy for the Jews suffering persecution under the Nazis. His own great-great-grandfather, Michael Benediks, had been one of the first Jews to settle in Sweden. Wallenberg was proud of his own Jewish blood. He began to feel frustrated with his business and his carefree life. With the coming of the war, there seemed much more important things to do. He imagined himself rescuing people, protecting them from harm or even death, and helping them to escape. Somehow and somewhere, he wanted to fight the Nazis.

OCCUPATION

On March 19, 1944, Hitler ordered his German troops to occupy Hungary. There was no fighting, as Hungary and Germany were still allies. But the Germans soon let everybody know who was in charge. German troops patrolled the streets and country roads. German tanks and artillery maneuvered in the outskirts of Budapest. Döme Sztójay, who was friendly with the Germans, became the prime minister. Germany ruled Hungary through its own ministers and diplomats. These officials arrived in Budapest to give the Hungarian government instructions straight from Adolf Hitler.

Döme Sztójay (*far left*), who served as Hungarian ambassador to Germany until he became prime minister of Hungary in 1944, was a supporter of Hitler's Nazi policies. He is seen here at a Nazi conference in Berlin, Germany, during the war.

German SS units went about their work in Hungarian towns and villages. Between May and July 1944, these units, under Adolf Eichmann's command, deported about 400,000 Jews from Hungary. They loaded their prisoners on approximately 148 freight trains and shipped them across Hungary's border with Poland. After several days, the trains arrived at Auschwitz. At this camp, prison guards killed thousands of Jews every day by poisoning them with gas. The bodies were burned in large ovens. Auschwitz became a factory of death.

The Nazis had laid out plans to make all of Europe *Judenrein*, or "free of Jews." They had almost succeeded in France, the Netherlands, Poland, and other nations they had

Hungarian Jews arrive at Auschwitz concentration camp in German-occupied Poland in 1944. Some historians today estimate that about half of all the Jews that were killed at Auschwitz (more than one million) were Jews from Hungary.

conquered. The majority of Jews living in these areas were now dead or imprisoned. Hungary represented the last obstacle to this goal. During the first four years of the war, Hungary had been a haven for Jews, even though Hungary had aligned with Germany. Jews from Romania, Czechoslovakia, and Poland had come in search of a safe place to live. Germany had demanded that Hungary deport its Jews and send them to the death camps. Nevertheless, until March 1944, the leaders of Hungary had refused to cooperate.

Hungary had passed many new laws against Jews, however. Jews were forced to sell farmland they owned. They were segregated from Christians at public events. Most could no longer obtain licenses to become doctors or lawyers. And those Jews who arrived in Hungary seeking a safe haven from the Nazis found that not even Hungary was safe. The Hungarian government allowed the Germans to send foreign non-Hungarian Jews to their deaths in Auschwitz.

For the task of making Hungary *Judenrein*, Germany sent Adolf Eichmann. Eichmann was a lieutenant colonel in the SS. For two years, he had been rounding up Jewish civilians, placing them on packed freight trains, and shipping them to concentration camps. Eichmann had destroyed Jewish communities in Austria, Germany, France, and Czechoslovakia. He hated Jews with a passion and felt proud of his accomplishments. In the spring of 1944, he turned to Hungary.

ADOLF EICHMANN

Adolf Eichmann was born on March 19, 1906, in Solingen, Germany. Before he became a member of the Nazi Party, Eichmann had a job as a salesman for an oil company and traveled in Upper Austria. He lost his work during the depression and joined the Nazis in 1932. He became a member of the SS and moved to Germany, where eventually he was appointed to the central office in Berlin to monitor Jewish activities. In 1938, after Germany annexed Austria, Eichmann organized a so-called central office for Jewish emigration in Vienna. This office coerced Jews to flee Austria by such means as terror, seizing their property, and threatening Jewish community leaders if they did not cooperate with him. He set up a similar office in Prague, Czechoslovakia, which became the model for the other territories that Germany occupied. Eichmann was involved with the expulsion of Jews from Poland beginning in 1939, and he was soon appointed as head of a section dealing with Jewish affairs. In 1942, at the Wannsee Conference (named after the Berlin suburb where the meeting was held), Nazi officials organized the methods they would use for the "final solution to the Jewish question." Eichmann was put in charge of the details, which attendees referred to as "the evacuation of the Jews to the East." His expertise in mass deportations expanded to include supervising the building of death camps and transporting millions of Jews to their deaths at Auschwitz, among other camps. Eichmann's role was the carrying out of policy, which he implemented with horrific efficiency.

By the summer, Eichmann had finished his task in the Hungarian countryside. But there were still more than 230,000 Jews living in Budapest. It was the last large community of Jews left in Nazi-occupied Europe. Eichmann was confident that he could make Budapest *Judenrein*. But he knew there was no time to waste. The armies of the Soviet Union were pushing back German units on the eastern front. In June 1944, the Allies—led by the United States—invaded northern France. Germany, as Eichmann and everyone else realized, was losing the war.

PRESIDENT ROOSEVELT CREATES THE WAR REFUGEE BOARD

In the United States, President Franklin D. Roosevelt and other government officials knew about the Nazi persecution of Jews in Europe. Reports had revealed that the Germans were forcing Jews out of their homes and putting them in concentration camps. The Germans were also setting up labor camps, where Jewish prisoners worked as slaves.

The United States had entered the war in December 1941. But for more than two years, the United States and the Allies did very little to stop the Nazi campaign against the Jews. There seemed more pressing goals to achieve, such as defeating

At the White House on December 11, 1941, President Franklin D. Roosevelt signs the declaration of war against Germany. After it became known that the Nazis were killing Jews in death camps, President Roosevelt established the War Refugee Board.

Germany and its ally, Japan, on the battlefield. The problem of Jewish civilians in occupied Europe seemed less important. There seemed to be little the United States could do.

But in the spring of 1944, two inmates of Auschwitz escaped the death camp. Newspapers throughout Europe and in the United States reported their stories. People realized there was more to this war than fighting battles. In countries they conquered, the Nazis were carrying out genocide. They were trying to destroy an entire population of Jewish civilians.

On January 22, 1944, President Roosevelt finally decided to take action against Nazi genocide in Europe by organizing the War Refugee Board (WRB) through Executive Order 9417. The order stated that "It is the policy of this government to take all measures within its power to rescue the victims of enemy oppression who are in imminent danger of death and otherwise to afford such victims all possible relief and assistance consistent with the successful prosecution of the war." The WRB would help rescue people threatened with deportation and the death camps. It would help them escape German-occupied countries and reach safe territory until the end of the war. The WRB helped Jews in Europe by giving them visas, which were documents that allowed them to move to the United States and other friendly countries. Members of the WRB also threatened Nazi leaders responsible for the persecution. They were warned that after the war, if they survived, they would be put on trial for their crimes.

After German troops occupied Hungary, the WRB turned its attention to the Hungarian Jews. Because the United States was at war with Hungary, which had been a German ally and now was occupied by Germany, the WRB asked Sweden and other neutral countries, including Switzerland, Spain, and Portugal, to send as many representatives as possible to Budapest. Neutral diplomats would serve as observers and, in any way possible, stop the Nazis from deporting Hungarian Jews. A representative of the WRB, Ivar Olsen, was living in Stockholm. The WRB asked Olsen to find a capable and courageous Swede, a diplomat who could travel to Budapest and rescue the Jews still living there. Although Hungary was allied to Germany, it allowed neutral Swedish diplomats to live and work in Budapest.

Olsen formed a committee of Swedish Jews. The committee set out plans for the rescue mission and began a search for its leader.

CHOOSING WALLENBERG

Koloman Lauer joined Olsen's committee. Because Lauer was a Hungarian and a Jew, Olsen asked him to take part in the search. On June 9, Lauer told Olsen that he knew just the man to help the WRB in its rescue mission. This man was a young Swede who could speak German and several other languages. Lauer had been impressed by the man's energy and intelligence and knew he could carry out this dangerous mission. In fact, Lauer's choice was one of his own business colleagues, the thirty-one-year-old salesman Raoul Wallenberg.

Olsen took Lauer's suggestion. The next night, Olsen, Lauer, and Wallenberg met to talk about the mission. It would mean a long trip through occupied territory. Wallenberg could expect tiring and frustrating work in a foreign city and much danger. Nevertheless, Wallenberg accepted the assignment right away.

The Swedish government, as well as the U.S. ambassador to Sweden, approved the selection of Wallenberg for the mission to Budapest. But Wallenberg set down his own conditions. If they were not met, he wouldn't take on the job. He must be able to move about, meet with whomever he wanted, and act independently of the Swedish embassy. He wanted to be appointed a first secretary. This position was a high official rank that would allow him to meet and deal with anyone he wanted, all the way up to the leaders of Hungary.

Wallenberg also wanted as much money as he might need to carry out his mission. He wanted the right to bribe officials whenever it might prove useful. He wanted the authority to buy buildings in Budapest and set up safe houses. He wanted to issue protective passes, which would be official Swedish documents and would allow the people holding them to escape arrest and deportation by the Germans or Hungarians.

Wallenberg made many other demands. The leaders of Sweden talked it over and passed the matter all the way up to the prime minister as well as the Swedish king, Gustav V. They accepted Wallenberg's conditions—he had proved himself a masterful negotiator.

The leaders of Sweden realized that they should cooperate with Wallenberg and the WRB. Although Sweden was neutral, the Swedes opposed Nazism. They also felt some shame for helping Germany early in the war. Sweden had traded its iron ore to Germany, and German factories had used it to make tanks, trucks, guns, and ammunition. Early in the war, Sweden had also allowed the German army to cross its territory to attack the Soviet Union. Now the Swedes wanted to do something to help the other side. Their humanitarian and rescue efforts would help aid victims of the war.

CHAPTER THREE

THE MISSION

Wallenberg prepared for his secret rescue mission by reading mail sent from diplomats who were working for the Swedish Foreign Ministry and living in Hungary. He also examined newspaper reports from central Europe. He discovered that the Germans had already sent several hundred thousand Jews out of Hungary to their deaths at Auschwitz and other camps.

Wallenberg realized that he had no time to lose. He left Sweden by plane for Berlin, Germany's capital, on July 6, 1944. In Berlin, he stayed with his half sister Nina, who was married to a Swedish diplomat. Wallenberg felt confident and eager to get to Budapest and get started.

It had been exactly one month since the invasion of France by the Allies. Since that time, the Germans had been pushed back in France and on the eastern front. The tide of the war had turned against them. Wallenberg realized that the Nazis would be stepping up their persecution of Jews in occupied territories.

They would be rushing to make Hungary and other countries in Europe *Judenrein* before the Allies could force their armies back into Germany. From Berlin, Wallenberg took a passenger train that was carrying German soldiers, who filled the halls and compartments of the train. Unable to find a seat, Wallenberg rested on the floor of a corridor. He carried nothing but the clothes on his back and a knapsack. Inside the knapsack he had packed a change of clothes, a bit of food, a gun, and a list of people in Budapest who might be able to help him. The southbound train passed another train heading north. This northbound train was carrying Hungarian Jews to Poland. On July 9, 1944—the same day that Wallenberg arrived in Budapest—the occupants of the train arrived at Auschwitz, where most would die.

A DIPLOMAT IN BUDAPEST

Wallenberg moved into a Swedish diplomatic house. He lived just a few streets away from the headquarters of the SS and Adolf Eichmann. Eichmann was angry and frustrated. The leader of Hungary, Miklós Horthy, had just asked the Germans to stop shipping Jews out of his country. The Hungarian police were no longer cooperating with Eichmann's men.

This photograph of Wallenberg was used for diplomatic identification while he was a Swedish special envoy in Budapest. Wallenberg arrived in Budapest on July 9, 1944.

Since March, Eichmann had made progress in Budapest. After his arrival, he had immediately asked the Hungarian government to pass new, stricter laws for Jewish citizens. Fearing that the Germans would take over their government completely, the Hungarians had agreed. All Jews in Budapest had to wear yellow stars that would identify them as being Jews. They could go outside their homes for only three hours each day. They could not own radios or telephones. The police closed down their businesses and banned them from attending schools, religious services, and public events. The police confiscated bicycles from adults and children.

In April 1944, the Hungarian police had begun herding the Jews of Budapest into schools, churches, synagogues, and houses marked with the yellow star. The yellow star made it easy for the police and the Germans to find and identify their Jewish targets. The Jews had no choice but to move into these crowded public places, where they often had little food to eat and not even a spot to lie down at night. Under Eichmann's orders, the Budapest Jews had also formed a Jewish council. Eichmann used the council to pass orders and instructions on to the Jewish community. He assured the members of the council that the Jews would be safe as long as they cooperated with him.

In May 1944, the trains began leaving Budapest, packed with Jews and headed for Auschwitz.

The overcrowded trains created problems for the commander of Auschwitz, Rudolf Hoess. Hoess could not keep up with the thousands of Jews who were arriving at his gates every day. The gas chambers worked overtime, yet the camp was overflowing with new arrivals. Hoess asked Eichmann to slow down the deportations from Hungary, but Eichmann felt determined to finish his job as soon as possible. He asked his own commander, Heinrich Himmler, the chief of the SS, for advice and orders.

The German army desperately needed trains for the transport of its equipment and for its soldiers. In answer to Eichmann, Himmler passed along an order directly from Adolf Hitler. The military could use any trains it wanted, as long as it was advancing. Retreating units would have to walk, if necessary. Because most German troops were now retreating, Eichmann found it easy to get as many trains as he needed. By July 6, the day Raoul Wallenberg left Stockholm, the deportations from the countryside were completed.

For that day, Eichmann had planned a grand roundup of all of the Jews in Budapest. Working together, German soldiers and Hungarian police would march the Jews to an island in the Danube, the river that runs through the middle of the city. From there, they would be sent to the city's train stations for the ride to Auschwitz. But then, Miklós Horthy gave his order stopping the roundup. Just before giving the order, he had sent 1,600 Hungarian policemen out of the city. The

Germans needed these men to help them round up the Jews. Even if Eichmann had ignored Horthy's orders, he would not have been able to carry out his plans.

Horthy was a naval war hero and a Hungarian patriot. At the beginning of World War II, he had decided to cooperate with Hitler and the Germans. As a reward, Germany had made parts of central Europe Hungarian territory. Hungary had lost this

Miklós Horthy, an admiral during World War I, is seen here on his white charger in Komorn, Hungary. Horthy, regent of Hungary from 1920 to 1944, worked with the Nazis, but he was anxious about how the Allies would deal with Hungary if Germany lost the war.

land by a treaty that was signed after World War I. Horthy admired the German government and felt a strong contempt for the Jews himself. But he also worried about the world's opinion of his country. Germany would probably lose the war. Hungary's future would depend on how much it cooperated with Eichmann and the SS. If the Hungarian leaders helped Eichmann commit his crimes, Horthy knew the Allies would hold them responsible.

THE *SCHUTZ-PASS*

After reaching Budapest, Wallenberg immediately set to work. He set up Section C, a special office within the Swedish embassy. Using money that the War Refugee Board had given him, he hired a large new staff. The members of his staff, most of whom were Jewish, prepared special passes for Jewish citizens. Already, the embassy had granted several hundred such passes to those who had business or family connections in Sweden. But only a tiny minority of Jews in Budapest could hope to get such a pass.

Wallenberg now set Section C to work full time to create new and more official-looking passes. Called the *Schutz-pass* ("Protection Pass"), Wallenberg helped design the pass and arranged to have each printed in blue and yellow on heavy paper. The passes carried photographs and official seals,

SCHUTZ-PASS Nr. 1/145

Name: Judith K o p s t e i n
Név:

Wohnort: Budgest
Lakás:

Geburtsdatum: 30. Jan 1930
Születési ideje:

Geburtsort: Budapest
Születési helye:

Körperlänge: 171 cm
Magasság:

Haarfarbe: blond Augenfarbe: blau
Hajszín: Szemszín:

Unterschrift:
Aláírás:

SCHWEDEN SVÉDORSZÁG

Die Kgl. Schwedische Gesandtschaft in Budapest bestätigt, dass der Obengenannte im Rahmen der — von dem Kgl. Schwedischen Aussenministerium autorisierten — Repatriierung nach Schweden reisen wird. Der Betreffende ist auch in einen Kollektivpass eingetragen.

Bis Abreise steht der Obengenannte und seine Wohnung unter dem Schutz der Kgl. Schwedischen Gesandtschaft in Budapest.

Gültigkeit: erlischt 14 Tage nach Einreise nach Schweden.

A budapesti Svéd Kir. Követség igazolja, hogy fentnevezett — a Svéd Kir. Külügyminisztérium által jóváhagyott — repatriálás keretében Svédországba utazik.

Nevezett a kollektív útlevélben is szerepel.

Elutazásáig fentnevezett és lakása a budapesti Svéd Kir. Követség oltalma alatt áll.

Érvényét veszti a Svédországba való megérkezéstől számított tizennegyedik napon.

Reiseberechtigung nur gemeinsam mit dem Kollektivpass. Einreisewisum wird nur in dem Kollektivpass eingetragen.

Budapest, den 20. August 1944

KÖNIGLICH SCHWEDISCHE GESANDTSCHAFT
SVÉD KIRÁLYI KÖVETSÉG

Kgl. Schwedischer Gesandte

Judith Kopstein's ***Schutz-pass***, or protection pass, is dated August 20, 1944. Wallenberg designed the passes to look very official, with the coat of arms of Sweden and diplomatic signatures and printed on heavy paper. The pass holder was to be under Swedish protection.

including the coat of arms of Sweden, and signatures. The writing stated that the holder would travel to Sweden after the war. Anyone having the pass was protected from being deported, arrested, or harmed in any way. The holder could also live in a special safe house under Swedish protection. Wallenberg convinced the Hungarian government to allow him to print 4,500 of them. A long line formed every day outside the doors of Section C on Minerva Street. Desperate men and women waited for hours, sometimes days, to receive their protective passes. They knew that the passport might help them to survive Eichmann's next roundup of Jews and, perhaps, the war.

Wallenberg also hired several hundred Budapest Jews as cooks, drivers, and assistants. He placed their families under the protection of the Swedish embassy. He set up medical clinics, arranged the distribution of food and medicine to Jewish families, and established soup kitchens.

In addition, he set up "safe houses" to shelter thousands of Jews within Budapest, protecting the houses with diplomatic immunity. Soon after Wallenberg arrived in Budapest, other neutral embassies—including those of Switzerland, Portugal, and Spain—began imitating his actions. They began issuing their own protective passes and setting up safe houses. Wallenberg worked hard, day and night. He was racing against time. While Section C prepared its special passes, Eichmann was demanding that the deportation of Jews resume.

The Guttmann family members, seen here wearing the yellow star designating them as Jews, survived the war by living in one of Wallenberg's safe houses in Budapest. Wallenberg made sure the houses were flying the Swedish flag, indicating neutral territory.

MAKING MORE DEMANDS

On August 1, 1944, Wallenberg met Miklós Horthy. He asked Horthy to expel Eichmann and the SS from Hungary. Two days later, Wallenberg met with the chief of Hungarian police. He also met with several

SAFE HOUSES

Wallenberg rented or bought about thirty-two city buildings using WRB funds and turned certain large houses in Budapest into safe houses. He arranged to buy or rent houses from Adolf Eichmann himself. Under Eichmann's orders, the Germans had seized many of these houses from their Jewish owners. Under Wallenberg's direction, the houses now belonged to Sweden, not to Hungary or to the Nazis. Each of them flew the Swedish flag. The flags meant the houses were neutral territory, protected from the police and German troops. They all served the same purpose—to shelter Jewish families from the Nazis and their northbound trains. Wallenberg's safe houses saved thousands of Jews from being killed or deported to Auschwitz.

other Hungarian officials. He made demands and gave warnings. He promised that if they continued helping the Nazis to persecute Jews, they would be arrested and put on trial for war crimes when the war ended. The Allies would throw them in prison or execute them. But he, Wallenberg, might be able to help them, if they helped him to protect the Jews.

Wallenberg's threats worked, for a time. But Eichmann also made threats. He surrounded the capital with SS units. He demanded that Horthy allow him to begin deportations again. He asked to deport at least fifty thousand more Jews out of the country. He set a new date for this action: August 25. Wallenberg heard about these plans. He wrote a strong letter to the Hungarian government and demanded that the Hungarians stop the deportations. His letter was also signed by ambassadors from Spain, Portugal, and Switzerland. The representative of the pope, the head of the Catholic Church, signed as well.

For the time being, the German government did nothing. Then, on August 24, Romania, another German ally, surrendered to the Soviet army. Romania had been an important source of oil for the Germans. Hungary also provided oil. The Germans wanted to keep control of Hungary's oil for the war effort. For now, the easiest way would be to stay friendly with Hungary's leaders. On August 30, Hungary and Germany reached an agreement. Germany would stop the deportations permanently. In exchange, Horthy agreed that the

Jews of Budapest would live in camps outside of Budapest, where they had to join forced-labor battalions. The Hungarians did round up groups of Jewish men to dig fortifications and trenches near Budapest. But Hungarian officials dragged their feet on expelling the Jews from the city. For another month, no Jews were sent out of Budapest.

In the meantime, the situation grew worse on the city's streets. Jews going out of doors, at any time of day, ran a very dangerous risk. The members of the Arrow Cross spent their time hunting down, beating, and killing Jews. Thousands of Jewish families searched desperately for an escape, but they found it impossible to leave the city. Police and soldiers blocked the roads and searched the trains. They checked all documents and sent back to Budapest Jews who were trying to flee. Some Jewish families hid in the homes of Christians who agreed to help them. Others tried to bribe officials for protection. Many Jews sought out foreign diplomats who they were

Arrow Cross Party members arrest Jews in Budapest near the end of 1944. A "reign of terror" against Jews intensified in Hungary after the Arrow Cross Party took charge of the government in October 1944.

told would give out false papers and passes to help shield them or would send them and their families to safe houses that were considered immune from the Nazi and Arrow Cross acts of deportation. Thousands came to the doors of the Swedish embassy, knowing that Wallenberg's special passports could help save their lives. Wallenberg and the embassy's actions and other foreign diplomatic offices rescued tens of thousands of Budapest's Jews.

CHAPTER FOUR

BARONESS ELISABETH KEMÉNY

The Germans were beginning to lose the war. Romania had surrendered, and the Soviets dictated the terms of a truce, which was signed in September 1944. The Soviet army had reached the border of Hungary and was preparing to attack Budapest. Hungary's leaders realized that the war was lost. They began looking for a way to make peace with the Allies. If Hungary stayed with Germany to the bitter end, the defeat might bring a hostile occupation of their country. They stopped cooperating with Eichmann's actions against the Jews.

For a time, Wallenberg believed the worst was over. Eichmann left the country, and the deportations stopped. Many Jews held protective passes, prepared in Section C of the Swedish embassy. The Hungarian government had agreed to reopen the city's synagogues. Jews were allowed outside their homes all day, like other citizens. Wallenberg cut his staff down to one hundred people. He prepared to end his mission and return home.

Meanwhile, the Soviet army continued its advance. Soviet troops and tanks reached the plains of central Hungary. By the end of September, the Germans had been pushed back even farther. Soviet troops came within fifty miles (80.5 kilometers) of Budapest. In early October, on Miklós Horthy's orders, Hungary made a secret agreement with the Soviet Union. Hungary would surrender to the Soviets on October 18. The Germans soon found out about the secret agreement. Suspecting this, Horthy decided to move faster than planned. On October 15—three days earlier than scheduled—he made a radio announcement. Hungary was withdrawing from the war immediately.

Horthy's radio announcement took many people by surprise—even his own generals in the Hungarian

Soviet tanks attack German defenses along the right bank of the Danube River as they approach Budapest in December 1944. Horthy secretly negotiated with the Soviets to surrender Hungary.

army. These Hungarian officers were not prepared to defend Budapest against the Germans and their allies in the Arrow Cross. On the same day, German and Arrow Cross soldiers moved into Budapest. They swarmed into government buildings. To assure Miklós Horthy's cooperation, they kidnapped his son and brought him to a prison camp inside Germany. Miklós Horthy agreed to submit to this coup d'état. Horthy fled Hungary. The leader of the Arrow Cross, Ferenc Szálasi, became the new Hungarian leader.

Eichmann returned to Budapest the day after the coup. He met with Hungary's new leaders. The Arrow Cross leaders were happy to give their full cooperation. They agreed to begin sending Jews out of Budapest again. Some would be sent to Germany right away as slave laborers. The rest would be brought to concentration camps near Budapest or herded into a ghetto in the middle of the city. The soldiers would seal off the ghetto and prevent anyone from leaving. Slave laborers would build a tall wooden wall, trapping the residents of the ghetto inside.

Eichmann also prepared a final plan to eliminate Budapest's Jewish population. The Arrow Cross and Hungarian police would collect the Jews of the ghetto and the labor camps. They would force the Jews to march to Hungary's border with Austria. There they would be put on trains and sent into Germany. To prevent any more problems or delay, the Arrow Cross announced that they would no longer respect protective passes of any kind.

THE ARROW CROSS TAKES CONTROL

Arrow Cross soldiers took over radio stations, police stations, and public buildings beginning in October 1944. Arrow Cross guards took control of the streets. They rounded up Jews, took them into jails and house cellars, and tortured them. They broke into safe houses and forced the occupants out at gunpoint. They killed Jews in cold blood in the streets and along the banks of the Danube.

At his home, Wallenberg learned that Arrow Cross soldiers had broken into his office. He immediately went to the office and ordered the soldiers to leave. He then went to Arrow Cross headquarters and demanded the release of his driver, who had been arrested. He spoke loudly and angrily in German. Unsure of how to deal with this commanding diplomat, who spoke the language of their German friends so well, the Arrow Cross soldiers and officers obeyed him.

Wallenberg ordered his staff to make up more protective passes. He decided to make as many as he needed. He would give them freely to anyone that wanted one. He drove around the city, keeping blank passes and a typewriter in his car.

Hundreds of Jews wait outside a branch of the Swiss consulate on Vadasz Street in Budapest hoping to obtain Swiss protection passes. Besides Sweden, Switzerland and other countries set up diplomatic havens to help shelter Jews and stop the deportations.

Whenever he found someone in trouble with the Germans or the Arrow Cross, he immediately made up a new pass for the person. He climbed out of his car, handed over the pass, and demanded the release of the prisoner. His confident demeanor and his command of German usually brought cooperation from anyone he encountered.

AN AUSTRIAN-BORN ALLY

After the Arrow Cross coup, Wallenberg knew he could not return home to Sweden yet. He searched for some new way to resist Eichmann. His passes and safe houses were no longer effective. He needed an ally with close connections to the new government. On October 18, he met that ally—a beautiful young woman named Baroness Elisabeth Kemény.

The baroness was wealthy and important. She had escaped Austria during the *Anschluss*, when Nazi Germany took over her homeland and annexed it in 1938. Like Wallenberg, she came from a well-known family. Her new Hungarian husband, Baron Gábor Kemény, served as the foreign minister in the Arrow Cross government. Although the baroness herself was born Jewish, she was baptized a Protestant, and her high status protected her from any harm by the Nazis or the Arrow Cross.

Soon after she married Baron Kemény, the baroness discovered that he was a Nazi sympathizer and an anti-Semite. The baroness felt anger and contempt toward her husband. She also detested Szálasi and the Arrow Cross government. She realized that Hungary had become nothing more than a puppet of Nazi Germany. When she met Wallenberg, she decided to help him in his mission to save the Jews. Wallenberg knew just what the baroness could do: persuade her husband to stop the deportations of the Jews. She could demand that his government recognize the protective passports. In return, Wallenberg promised to protect the baron from war crimes trials. These trials were sure to take place after the end of the war. He might save the baron's life. The baroness wanted to spare her husband from a trial and execution after the war. She was already pregnant with their first child. She wanted the child's father to survive the war.

Wallenberg also promised to ask Sweden to officially recognize the Hungarian government. Sweden would agree that Ferenc Szálasi and his ministers were the true rulers of Hungary. To Szálasi, this recognition was even more important than Baron Kemény's life. Szálasi and the other Arrow Cross leaders sought the world's respect. This respect might come with the formal recognition by Sweden and other nations. The baroness talked to the baron. Baron Kemény was a proud and devoted member of the Szálasi government. But he also felt love and devotion toward his

German chancellor Adolf Hitler (*center*) converses with Hungarian prime minister Ferenc Szálasi in Berlin in 1944. Wallenberg asked Baroness Kemény to persuade her husband to demand that Szálasi stop the deportation of Jews from Budapest.

young wife. He argued with the baroness, but he finally did as she asked. He persuaded Szálasi to stop the deportations—temporarily.

To carry out this decision, the baron read a proclamation over the radio, while Baroness Kemény stood at his side. He declared that the soldiers and police would not harm anyone holding protective passes. In addition, Jews no longer had to wear the yellow star. The special houses owned by Sweden and other neutral countries would again be safe from raids. The proclamation did not stop the violence in Budapest, though. The Arrow Cross soldiers were mostly young men. They represented the government in power, and they carried powerful automatic weapons. Few people had the authority or ability to stop them. Despite Kemény's proclamation, Arrow Cross men continued to arrest and torture many Jews and shot many others. Every day, they collected thousands of Jews and forced them to join work battalions. The Jewish laborers slaved in harsh conditions with no food or water. Many of them died after just a few days. Being forced into a work battalion was a sentence of death.

EICHMANN AND WALLENBERG'S MEETING

Every day, Wallenberg showed up in the square where the roundup of laborers took place. He ignored the guns and threats of the Arrow Cross guards. He shouted to the ragged, hungry, and frightened people in the crowds. Anyone holding a protective pass, he declared, should come forward. Anyone who had lost a pass should also step out of the crowd.

Hundreds of people obeyed Wallenberg's commands. They stepped out of the crowd, and away from certain death, even if they had never held a pass and they had no right to one. They realized Wallenberg was playing a trick on their guards. He didn't care if these Jews held passes or not. He didn't care about the rules and regulations set down for the passes. He gave out new passes to anyone who asked for one or who claimed to have lost one.

Meanwhile, Wallenberg made loud protests to the government. He complained about the roundup of slave laborers and about the shootings and torture carried out by the Arrow Cross. He promised that anyone harming Jews would be held responsible for their actions after the war. He sent messages and made phone calls to the highest ministers, even Szálasi himself.

Eichmann learned about Wallenberg's efforts to frustrate his plans. He grew angry and demanded that Wallenberg come to his office. Wallenberg agreed to his demand. His status as a diplomat protected him from the Nazis—or so he thought. The two men met at Eichmann's headquarters in the Majestic Hotel. They talked and argued bitterly. Wallenberg was calm, confident, and persuasive. He claimed that Germany would lose the war, and soon.

In reply, Eichmann decided to make an offer. In return for a large sum of money, the Germans would prepare a special train. Some—not all—of the Jews of Budapest could escape Hungary on this train.

Wallenberg promised to think about the offer. But he knew that he would never agree to it. He also knew that if some Jews were allowed to leave, the ones left behind would probably be killed. According to Alan Levy, in his book *Nazi Hunter: The Wiesenthal File* (revised edition, 2006), about the tireless work of Simon Wiesenthal to track down Nazi war criminals, when Eichmann was taking leave of Wallenberg, he supposedly said to Wallenberg, "I plan to do everything I can to keep you from saving your Jews. Your diplomatic passport won't protect you from everything. Even a neutral diplomat can meet with an accident." After the meeting with Wallenberg, Eichmann sent out orders to murder him.

CHAPTER FIVE

THE SOVIETS ENTER BUDAPEST

Baron Kemény had been persuaded by his wife to help Wallenberg stop the deportations of the Jews. It was November 19, 1944, and now the baron was furious. Sweden still had not recognized the Szálasi government, as Wallenberg had promised. Kemény sent a message to Wallenberg: If Sweden did not recognize his government by December 14, he would see to it that all the protections for the Jews would end. They would be rounded up, and the Arrow Cross and the SS units would kill them immediately or send them to Germany and certain death.

Despite Kemény's earlier radio proclamation, Eichmann was again sending Jews out of the city. His victims were forced laborers who were living in camps and factory yards in the outskirts of Budapest. SS and Arrow Cross troops marched their prisoners from these camps all the way to the town of Hegyashalom, on Hungary's border with Austria. The forced march took a full week, at the rate of twenty miles (about 32 km) every day. The marchers had no food, no water and no shelter. Along the way, thousands died of starvation, sickness, and exposure to the cold. Many others became too tired or sick to continue walking. Arrow Cross soldiers followed along, shooting anyone sitting or lying by the road. By the time the columns reached Hegyashalom, most of the people that had started out were already dead. At the border town of Hegyashalom, SS guards placed the survivors on trains. The trains brought them into Austria and then to Germany.

Wallenberg heard about the forced march to Hegyashalom. He drove out along the long columns of marchers. He delivered food and water where he could, and he rescued those marchers holding protective passes. He made loud protests to the guards and their officers along the road. He managed to stop hundreds of murders.

On November 23, Wallenberg drove all the way to Hegyashalom. He reached the train

Hungarian Jews are forced to work building bunkers, fortifications, and a spur for the railroad at Hajduhadhaz, a labor camp in eastern Hungary.

station with a few members of his staff. The SS guards did not stop him. Although they had lost the war and the Soviets were advancing, they still respected him as a neutral diplomat. Wallenberg ordered the guards to stand aside and allow him to find people holding protective passes. Hundreds of people already on the trains climbed out. Wallenberg began shouting out names. He used any common names that came to mind. He demanded that the named people come forward. Hundreds escaped the train, climbed onto waiting trucks, and returned to Budapest. Before Wallenberg left Hegyashalom that day, he unloaded a truckload of food. He asked the guards to give the food to the Jews still on the trains. It was all he could do for them.

CHAOS

By the end of November, as the Soviet army approached, Budapest was in chaos. Thousands of people fled the city. They packed into cars and trains and fled to the west, away from the Soviet soldiers. They knew that the Germans would fight for the city and that a terrible battle was about to take place.

Arrow Cross patrols searched out Jewish citizens in the streets and houses. As soon as they

Soviet soldiers fight the Germans in the streets of Budapest. The city was in complete confusion and disorder. Thousands escaped the city by fleeing west.

discovered a Jewish person, they began robbing and beating him or her. They led their victims into jails, where they tortured them for hours before killing them. They also marched hundreds of Jews to the banks of the Danube. They shot their victims as soon as they reached the river. To save bullets, they

Arrow Cross soldiers kill Jews along the banks of the Danube. Wallenberg frequently drove good swimmers and medical people to the Danube to help rescue any survivors who had been thrown into the river to be shot.

tied two or three victims together. They killed one prisoner and then shoved all of them into the freezing water. The living were dragged down into the river by the dead.

Wallenberg could do little to stop these acts. He recognized by now that his own life was in danger. There were orders out to kill him, by any means possible. His status as a diplomat would no longer protect him. One day, a German truck smashed into his car. Wallenberg realized that it wasn't an accident. Luckily, he had not been inside the car at the time. While diplomats of Sweden and other countries prepared their escape from Budapest, Wallenberg continued working to save the Jews.

On November 29, Baroness Kemény also prepared to leave. She was under suspicion for helping Wallenberg. One Arrow Cross official ordered her to be arrested. President Szálasi himself stopped the arrest. He demanded that she leave the country within one day. The baroness packed her bags and boarded a train for Italy. At the station to bid her farewell was Wallenberg. He and the baroness had become close friends.

THE LAST DAYS OF GERMAN OCCUPATION

In December, Eichmann ordered the remaining Jews of Budapest to be collected into the ghetto. The police and the Arrow Cross jammed thousands of Jews into houses and apartments. Crowds of hungry, desperate people lived in hallways, on staircases, and in basements. Others were not lucky enough to even have a roof over their heads. They lived in the streets and slept on the sidewalks. In the middle of December 1944, the Arrow Cross leaders of Hungary fled Budapest. On December 22, Eichmann also fled, along with the SS soldiers under his command. On the day after Christmas, the Soviets surrounded the

A SURVIVOR'S STORY

Agnes Mandl Adachi was born in Budapest in 1918. During World War II, she found refuge in the Swedish embassy in Budapest. She worked with Wallenberg in trying to save as many Jews as possible. After the Soviets came into Budapest, she left for Romania. She moved to Sweden, Australia, and the United States after the end of the war.

The following story is based on a 1992 interview with Agnes Mandl Adachi, and the transcript appears on the U.S. Holocaust Memorial Museum's online Holocaust Encyclopedia oral history web page (http://www.ushmm.org/wlc/en/media_oi.php?ModuleId=10005264&MediaId=1077).

The Blue Danube, which Agnes called the Red Danube because of all the Jewish blood that flowed there, separated the city of Budapest. The Hungarian Nazis typically roped three Jews together on the bank of the Danube, and shot the middle person so that all the people fell into the river. If the soldiers saw any movement in the water, they kept shooting until they were certain that the people were dead. It was a very cold winter near the end of 1944, and the river had "big slabs of ice." Wallenberg came to Agnes

and other Jews at the embassy and asked if anyone could swim. Agnes raised her hand and said, "Best swimmer in school." Wallenberg and the others, some of whom were doctors and nurses, went to the other side of the Danube that night, and the soldiers did not hear them because of the noise from the guns. Agnes and three men jumped into the Danube with ropes and helped save about fifty people until they could not stand the frozen water any more.

city and blocked all roads and railroad lines. Law and order came to an end in Budapest. Arrow Cross gangs roamed through the city, killing, robbing, and beating. Some historians estimate that between December 1944 and the end of January 1945, Arrow Cross soldiers took nearly twenty thousand Jews from the ghetto and murdered them.

Wallenberg continued issuing protective passes, sheltering Jews in safe houses, distributing food, and making protests to the Arrow Cross leaders who remained in the city. He bribed soldiers and policemen to prevent further roundups of Jews on the streets. He hid people in basements, attics, and even in the underground vault of a bank. Several times, he also stopped the Arrow Cross from herding more Jews into the crammed ghetto, where thousands of people were starving to death. In addition, he bribed regular Hungarian policemen to take people out of the ghetto and bring them to a safe house.

As the Soviet army drew closer to Budapest, the city grew more dangerous for Wallenberg. Nobody was safe, not even those who worked for the Swedish embassy. On January 7, Arrow Cross men attacked a safe house on Jokai Street that Wallenberg had set up. Neither the protective passes nor the Swedish flag flying over the house protected the inhabitants. Nearly three hundred people were taken out of the house, beaten, and marched away. The Arrow Cross forced many of their captives into work brigades. Within a few days, most of these laborers were murdered.

Knowing that the city would soon fall, the German and Arrow Cross officials prepared to kill all the people who remained inside the ghetto. SS officers drew up the plans. A machine-gun unit would assemble at the entrance to the Budapest ghetto. They would march inside and gun down the seventy thousand Jews still living within the ghetto walls.

As Soviet units advanced from the north, a friend of Wallenberg's, Pal Szalai, a disenchanted Arrow Cross official, learned about the mass murder that

would soon take place in the ghetto. Szalai was determined to stop it. He rushed to the Royal Hotel, where German soldiers, Arrow Cross units, and Hungarian policemen were gathering and preparing

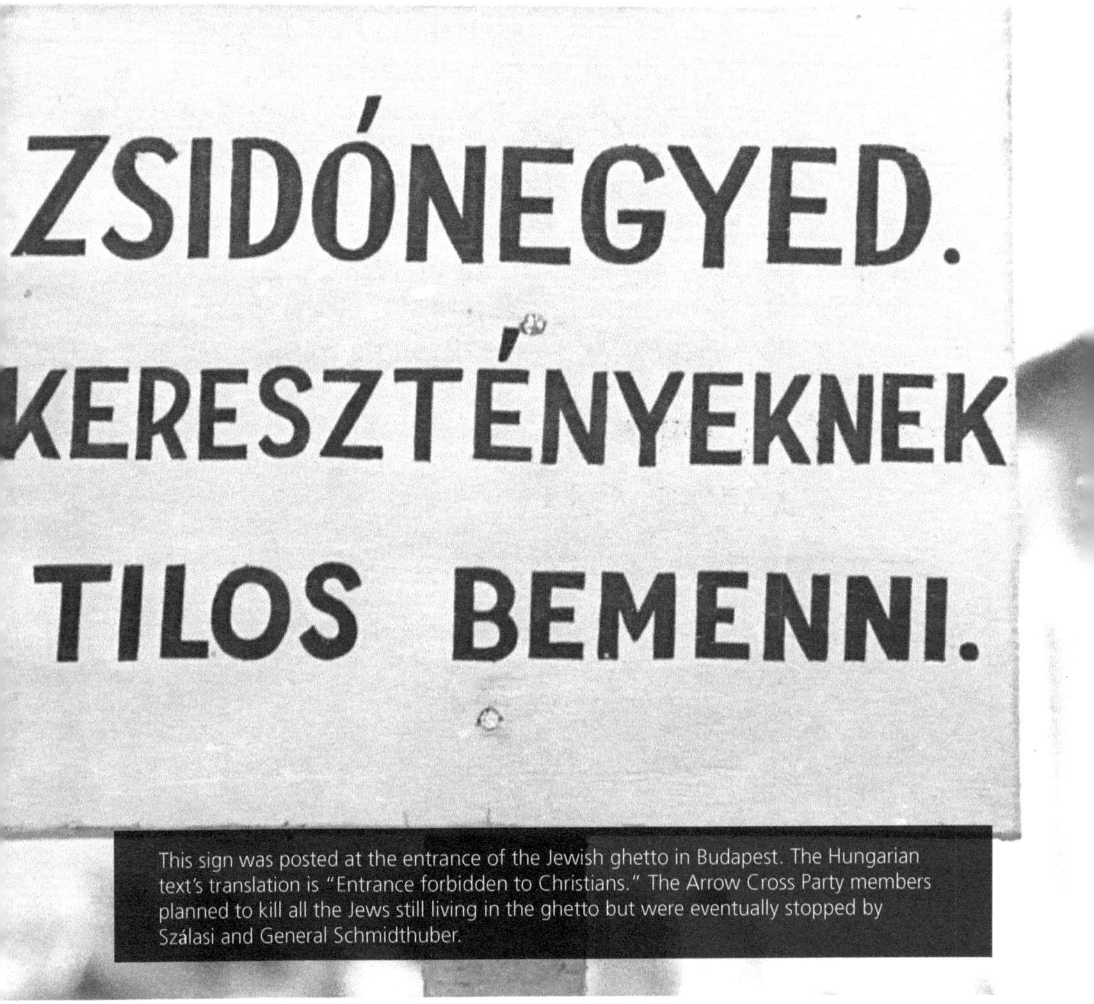

This sign was posted at the entrance of the Jewish ghetto in Budapest. The Hungarian text's translation is "Entrance forbidden to Christians." The Arrow Cross Party members planned to kill all the Jews still living in the ghetto but were eventually stopped by Szálasi and General Schmidthuber.

to take part in the massacre. Inside the hotel, Szalai found an SS general named August Schmidthuber. Szalai gave Schmidthuber a warning from Wallenberg. If the ghetto massacre took place, the general would be held personally responsible for it. He would be put on trial and probably executed as a war criminal.

Schmidthuber immediately called off the massacre after listening to Szalai. He ordered the German and Arrow Cross soldiers to stay away from the ghetto. Even though Wallenberg was not present, his threats prevented the murder of thousands of Jews in the ghetto. In all, about 120,000 Jews were still living in Budapest—in ghettos, hiding places, monasteries, convents, and various church basements. They made up more than half of the total Jewish population of the city before the war. Wallenberg helped save these people.

CHAPTER SIX

THE SOVIETS TAKE WALLENBERG PRISONER

The siege of Budapest raged. German and Hungarian troops battled desperately in the streets, even using the sewers to move troops. Tanks rumbled over barricades and trenches. Heavy Soviet guns shelled the city around the clock. To avoid the bloody and ruthless street fighting, thousands of Soviet soldiers advanced through underground tunnels and cellars toward the center of Budapest. It was now the second week of January 1945.

On January 10, Wallenberg drove to German army headquarters. He asked the Germans not to attack the safe houses where Jews and members of the Swedish embassy were now hiding from the fighting. On the next day, he finally

Budapest was severely damaged by bombs during the Soviet advance. In January 1945, Wallenberg moved to Benczur Street to meet the Soviets quickly so he could help Budapest's Jews.

took shelter in the cellar of a house on Benczur Street. The house was under the protection of the International Red Cross. Wallenberg knew that the house lay directly in the path of the advancing Soviet soldiers. He moved to Benczur Street because he wanted to meet the Soviets as soon as possible. Wallenberg understood that the fighting would soon end. The Germans would retreat, and the Soviets would win the battle for Budapest. He wanted the Soviets to help him get desperately needed food and medicine into the city after the fighting ended. He also wanted their support for his plans for the Hungarian Jews.

Wallenberg had been working on a new plan. After the war, he would establish the Wallenberg Institute for Support and Reconstruction. This organization would assist Jews in reuniting with their families. It would provide them with money, food, and housing if needed. It would help them find jobs. It would also give support to Jews who wanted to emigrate to Palestine, where Wallenberg expected a new Jewish homeland to be established. The Institute would use money from the U.S. War Refugee Board that was still available to Wallenberg. He would also raise money from wealthy Hungarians, from Swedes, and from anybody who had the ability to contribute.

On January 13, the Soviet army reached the house on Benczur Street. Major Dimitri Demchinkov arrived to talk to Wallenberg. Demchinkov took Wallenberg and his driver, Vilmos Langfelder, to his headquarters. There, Wallenberg asked permission to travel to the city of Debrecen, where the leader of the Soviet army directed the battle for Hungary. The NKVD, or Soviet secret police (a forerunner of the KGB), then took Wallenberg into custody. They questioned him for three days about his actions in Budapest. They allowed him to move around the city freely. But a three-man escort followed him everywhere he went.

When the Soviet army entered Bucharest, Romania, they were surrounded by hundreds of people greeting them as liberators. Nearly fifty thousand Soviets lost their lives fighting to liberate Budapest. The city was finally liberated on February 13, 1945.

Already, most of the employees of the Swedish embassy had escaped Hungary. The Soviets could not understand why Raoul Wallenberg had remained behind. They suspected that Wallenberg was some kind of spy. There seemed no good reason for him to stay in this dangerous city when nearly everyone who could leave had done so long ago.

ABDUCTED

On January 17, Wallenberg prepared to leave Budapest. Scattered fighting was still taking place in the city and in the surrounding countryside. But instead of returning to Sweden and safety, Wallenberg and Langfelder planned to drive to Debrecen. The Soviet commander, Marshal Rodion Malinovsky, had his headquarters there, and a group of Hungarians had formed a government. This government would be friendly to the Soviet Union. Its members would take power in Hungary after the war, under the watchful guidance of Soviet officers and troops.

Wallenberg wanted to meet Malinovsky and ask him to protect the Jews. He also wanted to persuade Malinovsky to help his postwar relief effort. He expected to return to Budapest after the meeting with Malinovsky. He had been dealing with the Nazis and their Hungarian allies since July 1944. He felt certain that he could also deal with the Soviets and that he could persuade them to cooperate with him. After all, the diplomats of Sweden had protected Soviet property in Budapest during the war. If necessary, Wallenberg would offer Malinovsky a bribe. He brought a large amount of money with him. He also ordered his driver to hide gold and jewelry in the gas tank of his car. These valuables had been given to him for safekeeping by Jewish and Christian families.

Outside of Budapest, a group of Soviet NKVD agents stopped Wallenberg's car. They ordered Wallenberg and Langfelder out of the car and arrested them. Essentially, they abducted them, taking them to Debrecen. Wallenberg still expected to meet Marshal Malinovsky. The meeting did not take place. Instead, the NKVD put Wallenberg and Langfelder on an eastbound train. For two weeks, the train proceeded through Eastern Europe, through Romania, the Ukraine, and Russia. Finally, on January 31, 1945, it reached Moscow, the capital of the Soviet Union.

The Soviet police supposedly brought Wallenberg and Langfelder to Lubyanka, a huge gulag, or prison, and police headquarters in central Moscow. Here the NKVD held and interrogated thousands of prisoners. Many of them were foreigners like Wallenberg. They were Austrians, Germans, Italians, and Swiss, and there were even a few Americans. The Soviets accused these prisoners of being spies. Most of them would be released after the end of the war.

ANNE APPLEBAUM'S *GULAG: A HISTORY* (2003)

Anne Applebaum is a columnist who writes about foreign affairs for the *Washington Post*. In 2004, Applebaum received a Pulitzer Prize for General Nonfiction for her book entitled *Gulag: A History*. After the end of the Soviet Union in 1991, access to some archives and memoirs have enabled people to research historical resources and study the role of the Soviet gulag (an acronym for Glavnoe Upravlenie Lagerei, or Main Camp Administration, the establishment that ran the Soviet camps) since the Russian Revolution in 1917.

Applebaum explained that the gulag was a flexible term for a variety of detainment and penal camps. A gulag could be a labor camp, a punishment camp, a camp in which criminals and political enemies were imprisoned, a women's camp, a children's camp, a transit camp—it signified the system of Soviet slave labor.

In the book, she made it clear that although the tsars had forced labor camps throughout Russian history, it wasn't until Vladimir Lenin and the Bolsheviks created the first Soviet concentration camps in 1918 and used police terror that the gulag became intertwined with the Soviet state. The first mass executions were also conducted at that time. Under Joseph Stalin, at the end of the 1920s, the labor camp system had been completely established.

Applebaum estimated that from 1929 through 1953 more that eighteen million people were placed in camps, with an additional six million being exiled to distant regions of the Soviet Union. Most of these people had done nothing wrong or were enemy combatants who were supposed to be treated humanely according to international agreements governing the treatment of prisoners of war. Of the 18 million inmates, about 4.5 million never returned to their homes.

Applebaum also described the conditions in the camps, which were supposed to be extreme but not unbearable. The gulag became "over time, a country within a country, almost a separate civilization, with its own laws, customs, literature, folklore, slang, and morality." During World War II, the destructive camp system reached its peak. Almost a quarter of the inmates died in 1942.

After the war, all kinds of inmates, including German prisoners of war, anti-Communists, Japanese troops, and certain nationalities, deluged the camps. It was not until 1953 that the labor camps began to free inmates. As of 2015, there still has been no official proof offered to Swedish or American authorities or to Raoul Wallenberg's family that Wallenberg died of a heart attack in July 1947 while confined in Lubyanka Prison.

A MYSTERIOUS FATE

Meanwhile, the war went on in Hungary. Soviet and German soldiers fought in Budapest until the end of February 1945. Soviet control did not bring safety to the people of the city. Soviet soldiers broke into houses, beating the inhabitants and stealing money and valuables. There was little food, and thousands of people were starving.

Wallenberg's family feared for his safety. A story about Wallenberg appeared in a leading Swedish newspaper. For the first time, the people of Sweden learned who Raoul Wallenberg was and what he had done during the war. Swedish leaders began asking questions about Wallenberg. Where was he? Why had the Soviets abducted him and apparently taken him back to a Soviet gulag? When would they release him?

RIVALS IN THE COLD WAR

Soviet prison officials allegedly asked Wallenberg many questions about his activities in Budapest. The war in Europe ended in May 1945. The war between the United States and Japan ended in August. But the end of the fighting did not bring Raoul Wallenberg his freedom. The Soviets did not release him from prison. They did not believe his stories and explanations. Wallenberg, a member of a rich Swedish family, would never live in a dangerous place such as Budapest and spend his time saving Jews, or so they thought. Wallenberg must have been up to something very different during the war. His position as a Swedish diplomat was just a trick, a cover for a very different job.

The Soviets believed that the Germans were using Wallenberg as a spy. If not the Germans, then the Americans. Although the United States and the Soviet Union were allies during the war, they were also rivals with very different political and economic systems. After World War II, they would become the world's two most powerful nations. These two superpowers would fight the Cold War around the world. Wallenberg, because he had once lived in the United States, came under suspicion. By interrogating Wallenberg's friends after the war, Soviet officials also learned that he had been hired by the WRB, an agency of the United States government. In the eyes of Soviet officials, this made him their enemy.

THE SEARCH CONTINUES

In the meantime, Wallenberg's family was still trying to free him from the Soviet Union. His mother made many phone calls and wrote countless letters to Swedish officials. But the many questions about Wallenberg began to anger Soviet officials. With the liberation of Hungary in 1945, the new Soviet-controlled government announced on the radio in March 1945 that Wallenberg probably had been killed by Hungarian Nazis or German SS agents on January 17, 1945, the day he had set out for Debrecen with Vilmos Langfelder. Sweden's ambassador in the Soviet Union believed that Wallenberg was dead. However, most of the general public did not believe the radio announcement.

Sweden did not press the matter of Wallenberg. Compared to the Soviet Union, Sweden was a small and very weak country. The Swedes did not want to anger Soviet officials by asking too many questions. After all, millions of people had died during the war. Millions more were missing and probably dead. Wallenberg might be one of them. One young diplomat, no matter what he had done to help the Jews of Budapest, did not seem worth all the trouble.

Finally, on August 18, 1947, the Soviet official Andrei Vyshinsky made a statement. He claimed that Wallenberg had never been in the Soviet Union. He also claimed there were no records of Wallenberg. Soviet authorities had searched the prisoner of war (POW) ward camps and other gulags and found no trace of Wallenberg. Vyshinsky said Wallenberg had probably died at the hands of German or Hungarian Nazis during the fighting for Hungary.

Throughout the mid 1940s to the early 1950s, various diplomats and Soviet and German prisoners who were released from Soviet camps told

Wallenberg's half sister Nina Lagergren holds a photo of Wallenberg at her apartment near Stockholm, Sweden. His family has never stopped trying to get the truth about what happened to Wallenberg after he was abducted by the Soviets.

of being held in a cell with Wallenberg or in one nearby at some point in their imprisonments. The Swedish government demanded explanations and additional information on Wallenberg. Apparently, Soviet officials did not want the world to know that Wallenberg might still be alive.

On February 6, 1957, the Soviet government finally gave a direct answer to the many appeals made for information on Raoul Wallenberg. An official memorandum declared that on July 17, 1947, Colonel A. L. Smoltsov, the head of the prison hospital service at Lubyanka, reported that Wallenberg had died suddenly the night before of a heart attack. He would have been thirty-five years old the following month. From that time on, the Soviets gave the same answer every time they were asked about Wallenberg's fate. Few people outside the Soviet Union believed it. Many Soviet prisoners throughout the 1950s claimed to have met Wallenberg (others referred to "a Swede"), either in a jail cell or during transportation from one prison to the next. Their reports appeared in books and newspaper stories throughout the late 1950s.

The Cold War between the United States and the Soviet Union dragged on. The two superpowers were fighting for allies in Europe, Africa, and Asia. The imprisonment of one man seemed to matter very little. Sweden and the United States demanded information, but when Soviet officials refused to give it, the matter was dropped.

SOME RECOGNITION

Yad Vashem of Israel, a living memorial to the Holocaust and a center of research and education, recognized Wallenberg as one of The Righteous Among the Nations on November 26, 1963. This tribute pays honor to the people who stood by Jews at a time of persecution and horrific tragedy.

In 1981, U.S. President Ronald Reagan signed a law that made Raoul Wallenberg an honorary U.S. citizen. The people of Budapest raised a memorial in honor of Wallenberg and his mission to their city, and named a street after him.

With the formal collapse and breakup of the Soviet Union in December 1991, a new government came to power in Russia, the largest of the now independent former Soviet republics. Still, Wallenberg did not appear. The new government gave out no new information about him or his fate. If he was still alive, he would have been seventy-nine years old and would have spent forty-six years in Soviet prisons. If he was dead, there were no reliable reports about when or how he had died, or where he was buried.

In 2009, journalist Joshua Prager reported in an article in the *Wall Street Journal* that in February 1979 Wallenberg's mother and stepfather committed suicide because they were distraught about being unable to bring their son home. In August 2009, Guy von Dardel, Wallenberg's half brother

The Raoul Wallenberg Holocaust Memorial Park in Budapest commemorates Wallenberg and the others who protected Jews in Budapest. The sculpture of the tree of life (a willow tree, a traditional symbol of mourning) honors the five thousand victims of the Holocaust who are buried nearby.

passed away. His family members said that they would continue the life-long goal to bring Wallenberg back home.

The government of Sweden made the year 2012 "Raoul Wallenberg Year" on the centennial

of Wallenberg's birth. It also announced that it would reopen an inquiry into the Wallenberg case. As of 2015, there has been no change in the official Russian stance, that Wallenberg had died of a heart attack in July 1947.

NEW RESEARCH

According to a report by the British Broadcasting Corporation (BBC) in February 2015, two U.S.-based researchers who were investigating Wallenberg's death received a letter in 2009 from Russia's secret police, the Federal Security Service (FSB). The letter stated that it was likely that Wallenberg had been renamed "Prisoner No. 7" and that documents existed that this prisoner had been interrogated for sixteen hours at Lubyanka on July 23, 1947—that was six days after Wallenberg's supposed death by a heart attack. There were also numerous reports from other prisoners, including jailed diplomats, that they had seen a Swede who looked like Wallenberg and who had called himself by that name. Some of these former prisoners insisted that they saw Wallenberg in prison many years after 1947. Although these so-called appearances throughout the 1950s have been investigated, no definitive proof of Wallenberg's being alive at these times has surfaced.

Even Wallenberg's family, particularly Marie Dupuy, the daughter of Guy von Dardel, continued to search for information about the circumstances surrounding Wallenberg's disappearance. According to Dupuy, the report that Wallenberg was "Prisoner No. 7" had not been confirmed by any documentation yet provided to the family. As of 2015, the family has not been given access to any proof of Wallenberg's disappearance, death, or even that he was interrogated for more than sixteen hours on July 23, 1947, at Lubyanka. However, the family received a censored copy of a page documenting that two other prisoners had been questioned along with Prisoner No. 7 on the same day. These prisoners were Wallenberg's driver, Vilmos Langfelder, and Langfelder's cellmate, Sandor Katona. It is based on this information that the FSB believed that Prisoner No. 7 was in all probability Wallenberg. But the FSB refused to give Wallenberg's family a copy of the entry for Prisoner No. 7 as it appears in the interrogation register at Lubyanka, nor did the FSB allow any of the U.S.-based researchers to review this page in the register. Although Dupuy has filed her own requests to review documentation over the years, the FSB has not allowed such access. Furthermore, Swedish, American, and Hungarian politicians and diplomats have not been able to confirm, without any doubt, what actually happened to Raoul Wallenberg after his arrival at Lubyanka.

After spending a few dangerous months saving thousands of people from death at the hands of the Nazis, Raoul Wallenberg had disappeared, supposedly a prisoner of the Soviet government and a victim of the Cold War. Nevertheless, his name and his deeds survived. Today he is remembered throughout the world as one of the great heroes of World War II. Numerous books have been published about him, and movies about Wallenberg and his mission continue to be produced. Journalist Tom Teicholz wrote in *Forbes* magazine in April 2015, "Wallenberg continues to hold the imagination of readers as much as writers because he was like a shooting star, or a passing comet: a source of light in very dark times that disappeared far too soon after his brilliance."

TIMELINE

August 4, 1912 Raoul Gustav Wallenberg is born near Stockholm, Sweden.

1931 Wallenberg journeys to the United States and enrolls at the University of Michigan in Ann Arbor to study architecture.

1935 Wallenberg graduates from the University of Michigan in Ann Arbor; his grandfather sends him to South Africa to become a businessman.

September 1, 1939 Germany attacks Poland, beginning World War II.

1940 Wallenberg goes to work as a salesman for the Central European Trading Company.

1941 Wallenberg travels and witnesses the Nazi occupation of Europe.

January 1944 President Franklin D. Roosevelt establishes the War Refugee Board to help people fleeing Nazi-occupied countries.

March 19, 1944 German troops occupy Hungary.

May 1944 Deportation of Hungarian Jews to the concentration camp Auschwitz begins.

July 7, 1944 Wallenberg leaves Berlin, Germany, for Hungary.

July 9, 1944 Wallenberg arrives in Budapest.

July 19, 1944 He meets Adolf Eichmann at the Majestic Hotel in Budapest.

October 1944 The Hungarian government tries

to sever ties with the Nazis and is overthrown by fascist extremists.

December 1944 Eichmann and his SS troops flee Budapest as the Soviets surround the city.

January 1945 Soviet troops enter Budapest. Soviet secret police arrest Wallenberg on January 17. He supposedly is later transferred to Lubyanka Prison, in Moscow. He is never heard from again.

1957 The Soviet government officially releases a statement that a document dated July 17, 1947, from the head of the Lubyanka prison hospital service reported that Wallenberg died of a heart attack the night before.

November 26, 1963 Yad Vashem of Israel names Wallenberg as Righteous Among the Nations.

1981 President Ronald Reagan signs a law making Wallenberg an honorary citizen of the United States.

1995 A bronze portrait bust of Raoul Wallenberg, sculpted by Miri Margolin, is donated to the United States Congress and is located in Emancipation Hall in the U.S. Capitol Visitor Center in Washington, D.C.

January 2012 Sweden announces that 2012 is officially Raoul Wallenberg Year, in honor of the centennial of his birth; Sweden reopens an inquiry into the Wallenberg disappearance case.

July 9, 2014 Wallenberg is posthumously awarded a Congressional Gold Medal during a ceremony in the U.S. Capitol Rotunda in recognition of his achievements and heroic actions during the Holocaust.

2015 Wallenberg's family continues to seek documents that fully disclose what happened to Wallenberg after the Soviets arrested him in January 1945.

GLOSSARY

abduct To kidnap or capture someone.

Allies The group of nations fighting the Axis powers of Germany, Italy, and Japan during World War II. The United States, Great Britain, France, and the Soviet Union all belonged to the Allies.

alumnus A male graduate or former student of a school or university.

Anschluss The political union and annexation of Austria by Nazi Germany in 1938.

anti-Semite An individual who fears and hates Jewish people and the Jewish religion.

Arrow Cross (Nyilas) A Hungarian political party closely allied with the Nazi Party of Germany.

Auschwitz A prison camp set up by the Germans in southern Poland during World War II. The Germans gathered civilians, mostly Jews, from all over central Europe and sent them to Auschwitz to be murdered.

Axis A word indicating Nazi Germany and its allies during World War II.

Bolshevik Communist.

coerce To make a person do something against his or her will through physical force or threat.

Cold War The worldwide rivalry between the United States and the Soviet Union that began after their common victory over Nazi Germany in World War II.

concentration camp A prison camp in which opponents of the Nazis were held without trial.

coup d'état The sudden overthrow of an established government by its opponents.

deportation The action of expelling or banishing a foreigner from a country.

diplomatic immunity The privilege of being free from arrest, taxation, payment of customs fees, and certain other laws, usually granted to diplomats by the country in which they are working.

execution The act of putting to death, often as punishment for a crime or in accordance with the law.

genocide The deliberate and systematic destruction of a racial, national, or cultural group.

ghetto During World War II, a neighborhood forcibly set up by Nazi occupation forces for Jewish citizens.

gulag A camp such as a labor camp that existed in the Soviet Union and that often held political prisoners, many of whom died.

Jewish council A committee of leading Jewish citizens, set up and controlled by Nazi occupation forces to control Jewish civilians.

Judenrein A German word meaning "free of Jews." It was the goal of Nazi Germany to make all areas occupied by its armies *Judenrein*.

Nazi Party A political party, the National Socialist German Workers' Party, led by Adolf Hitler that took power in Germany in 1933.

NKVD The secret police force of the Soviet Union, used to arrest and imprison Soviet enemies during World War II.

persecution The act of mistreating someone because of his or her race or political or religious beliefs.

Schutz-pass A "protection pass" that Raoul Wallenberg issued to Jews to protect them from deportation from Budapest.

***Schutztaffel* (SS)** A special branch of the military services of Nazi Germany. The SS dealt with the control and persecution of people living under Nazi occupation, especially the Jews, and administered the concentration camps.

Section C A special department of the Swedish embassy in Budapest, Hungary. Raoul Wallenberg used Section C to issue protection passes and assist Hungary's Jews.

segregate To separate people because of their race, sex, or religion.

War Refugee Board A department of the U.S. government, set up to protect persecuted civilians in Europe during World War II.

FOR MORE INFORMATION

Holocaust Memorial Center
Zekelman Family Campus, 28123 Orchard Lake Road
Farmington Hills, MI 48334
(248) 553-2400
Website: http://www.holocaustcenter.org
This center has a museum and archival research resources, including an oral history collection, and has been teaching about the Holocaust for more than twenty-five years.

The International Raoul Wallenberg Foundation
34 East 67th Street
New York, NY 10065
(212) 737-3275
Website: http://www.raoulwallenberg.net
This foundation works to establish educational programs and public awareness campaigns about "the values of solidarity and civic courage, ethical cornerstones of the Saviors of the Holocaust." It has offices in New York, Jerusalem, Buenos Aires, Berlin, and Rio de Janeiro.

Museum of Jewish Heritage
36 Battery Place
New York, NY 10280
(646) 437-4202
Website: http://www.mjhnyc.org/findex.html

Created as a memorial to those who perished in the Holocaust, this museum honors those who died by celebrating their lives, the traditions that they embraced, and their achievements and faith.

Raoul Wallenberg Committee of the United States
37 West 26th Street, Suite 403
New York, NY 10010
(646) 678-3711
Website: http://www.raoulwallenberg.org
This committee was created in 1981 to provide the American public with information about the heroic and humanitarian mission of Raoul Wallenberg. It also supports efforts to find out about Wallenberg's fate and bestows the Raoul Wallenberg Award and the Civic Courage Award on people, communities, and organizations that mirror Wallenberg's humanitarian and courageous works.

Sarah and Chaim Neuberger Holocaust Education Centre
UJA Federation of Greater Toronto
Lipa Green Centre, Sherman Campus
4600 Bathurst Street, 4th Floor
Toronto, ON M2R 3V2
Canada
(416) 631-5689
Website: http://holocaustcentre.com/
A part of the Jewish Museum of Canada, the Neuberger Holocaust Education Centre houses

a museum, provides educational resources, preserves survivor testimonies, and sponsors programs that foster understanding and dialogue about the Holocaust.

The Simon Wiesenthal Center
1399 South Roxbury Drive
Los Angeles, CA 90035
(310) 553-9036
Website: http://www.wiesenthal.com
This organization works internationally for human rights and researches the Holocaust, fights anti-Semitism, hate, and terrorism, and safeguards the safety of Jews around the world. It maintains three Museums of Tolerance, produces films, and offers a massive library of information about the Holocaust.

USC Shoah Foundation
The Institute for Visual History and Education
650 West 35th Street, Suite 114
Los Angeles, CA 90089-2571
(213) 740-6001
Website: http://sfi.usc.edu/
The Shoah Foundation is a research and education institution that seeks "to overcome prejudice, intolerance, and bigotry" by capturing and preserving video testimonies of survivors of the Holocaust. The foundation also includes testimonies of survivors of genocides other than the Holocaust.

United States Holocaust Memorial Museum
100 Raoul Wallenberg Place, SW
Washington, DC 20024-2126
(202) 488-0400
Website: http://www.ushmm.org/
This museum is “a living memorial” to the Holocaust by encouraging people worldwide to confront hatred, stop genocide, and promote human dignity. It is located on the National Mall in Washington and offers a narrative history of the Holocaust, historical exhibits, and videos that include personal survival stories.

Vancouver Holocaust Education Centre
50–950 West 41st Avenue
Vancouver, BC V5Z 2N7
Canada
(604) 264-0499
Website: http://www.vhec.org/about.html
The Vancouver Holocaust Education Centre is a teaching museum that offers online and site-based exhibits, educational programs and materials, and cultural and commemorative events that encourage awareness of discrimination and racism through remembrance of the Holocaust.

Yad Vashem
The Holocaust Martyrs’ and Heroes’ Remembrance Authority
P.O. Box 3477
Jerusalem 9103401

Israel
972-2-6443574
Website: http://www.yadvashem.org
This organization is committed to commemorate, document, research, and educate the public about the Jewish people and the Holocaust. Its website includes information on the Holocaust, survivor stories, digital collections, photo archives, online exhibitions, and many other educational materials.

WEBSITES

Because of the changing nature of Internet links, Rosen Publishing has developed an online list of websites related to the subject of this book. This site is updated regularly. Please use this link to access the list:

http://www.rosenlinks.com/HOLO/Wall

FOR FURTHER READING

Applebaum, Anne. *Gulag: A History*. E-book. New York, NY: Anchor eBooks, 2010.

Bierman, John. *Righteous Gentile: The Story of Raoul Wallenberg, Missing Hero of the Holocaust*. Rev. ed. Harmondsworth, UK: Penguin Books, 1995.

Bitton-Jackson, Livia. *I Have Lived a Thousand Years: Growing Up in the Holocaust*. New York, NY: Simon Pulse, 2009.

Borden, Louise W. *His Name Was Raoul Wallenberg: Courage, Rescue, and Mystery During World War II*. Boston, MA: Houghton Mifflin Harcourt, 2012.

Brezina, Corona. *Nazi Architects of the Holocaust* (A Documentary History of the Holocaust). New York, NY: Rosen Publishing, 2015.

Chiga, Krystyna, and Daniel Paisner. *The Girl in the Green Sweater: A Life in Holocaust's Shadow*. New York, NY: St. Martin's, 2012.

Darman, Peter. *The Holocaust and Life under Nazi Occupation*. New York, NY: Rosen Publishing, 2012.

Deem, James. *Auschwitz: Voices from the Death Camp*. Berkeley Heights, NJ: Enslow Publishers, 2011.

Down, Susan Brophy. *Irena Sendler: Bringing Life to Children of the Holocaust*. New York, NY: Crabtree Press, 2012.

Freedman, Jeri. *The Warsaw Ghetto and Uprising (A Documentary History of the Holocaust)*. New York, NY: Rosen Publishing, 2015.

Jangfeldt, Bengt. *The Hero of Budapest: The Triumph and Tragedy of Raoul Wallenberg*. London, UK and New York, NY: I.B. Tauris, 2014.

Kershaw, Alex. *The Envoy: The Epic Rescue of the Last Jews of Europe in the Desperate Closing Months of World War II*. Cambridge, MA: Da Capo Press, 2010.

Levine, Paul A. *Raoul Wallenberg in Budapest: Myth, History and Holocaust*. London, UK and Portland, OR: Vallentine Mitchell, 2010.

Marton, Kati. *Wallenberg: The Incredible True Story of the Man Who Saved the Jews of Budapest*. New York, NY: Arcade, 2011.

Ozsváth, Zsuzsanna. *When the Danube Ran Red*. Syracuse, NY: Syracuse University Press, 2010.

Rosenfeld, Harvey. *Raoul Wallenberg: The Mystery Lives On*. Lincoln, NE: iUniverse, 2005.

Wallenberg: A Hero's Story. DVD. Paramount Home Entertainment, 2011.

Weale, Adrian. *Army of Evil: A History of the SS*. New York, NY: NAL Caliber, 2012.

INDEX

S

U

V

W

ABOUT THE AUTHORS

Emma Simon is a descendant of German immigrants and grew up in a small farm town in Michigan. She has studied the Holocaust for many years, and this is her first collaboration on a book for young people.

Tom Streissguth was born in Washington, D.C., and raised in Minneapolis, Minnesota. He has traveled widely in Europe and the Middle East and has worked as an editor, journalist, and teacher. He has written numerous nonfiction books on biography, geography, and history for young adults.

PHOTO CREDITS

Cover AFP/Getty Images; p. 5 Ryan Donnell/Aurora//Getty Images; pp. 6-7 (background) Ingo JezierskiPhotographer's Choice/Getty Images; pp. 6-7 (inset) Andrew Francis Wallace/Toronto Star/Getty Images; pp. 11, 24, 40, 55, 67, 79 Rolf E. Staerk/ Shutterstock.com; pp. 12-13, 21, 35, 45 © AP Images; p. 15 Keystone/Hulton Archive/Getty Images; pp. 18-19 Fox Photos/Hulton Archive/ Getty Images; p. 25 Photo 12/Universal Images Group/Getty Images; pp. 26-27 Keystone-France/Gamma-Keystone/Getty Images; pp. 29, 63 ullstein bild/Getty Images; pp. 30-31 Galerie Bilderwelt/Hulton Archive/Getty Images; p. 42 © Everett Collection Historical/Alamy; p. 47 Apic/Hulton Archive/Getty Images; p. 49 United States Holocaust Memorial Museum, courtesy of Irving and Emma Eisner; pp. 52-53 United States Holocaust Memorial Museum, courtesy of Eva Hevesi Ehrlich; pp. 56-57, 70-71, 81 Sovfoto/Universal Images Group/ Getty Images; pp. 60-61 United States Holocaust Memorial Museum, courtesy of Agnes Lutz Hirschi; pp. 68-69 United States Holocaust Memorial Museum, courtesy of John Gerrard; p. 72 United States Holocaust Memorial Museum; pp. 76-77 United States Holocaust Memorial Museum, Magyar Nemzeti Muzeum Torteneti Fenykeptar, courtesy of Lilly Brust-Gach; p. 79 (inset) Hulton Archive/Archive Photos/Getty Images; p. 89 Jonathan Nackstrand/AFP/Getty Images; pp. 92-93 Insights/Universal Images Group/Getty Images; interior pages background textures and graphics Aleksandr Bryliaev/Shutterstock.com, kak2s/Shutterstock.com, argus/Shutterstock.com, Sfio Cracho/Shutterstock.com; back cover Ventura/Shutterstock.com.

Designer: Michael Moy; Editor: Kathy Kuhtz Campbell; Photo Researcher: Carina Finn

SPORTS TO THE EXTREME™

ROCK AND ICE CLIMBING

Therese Shea

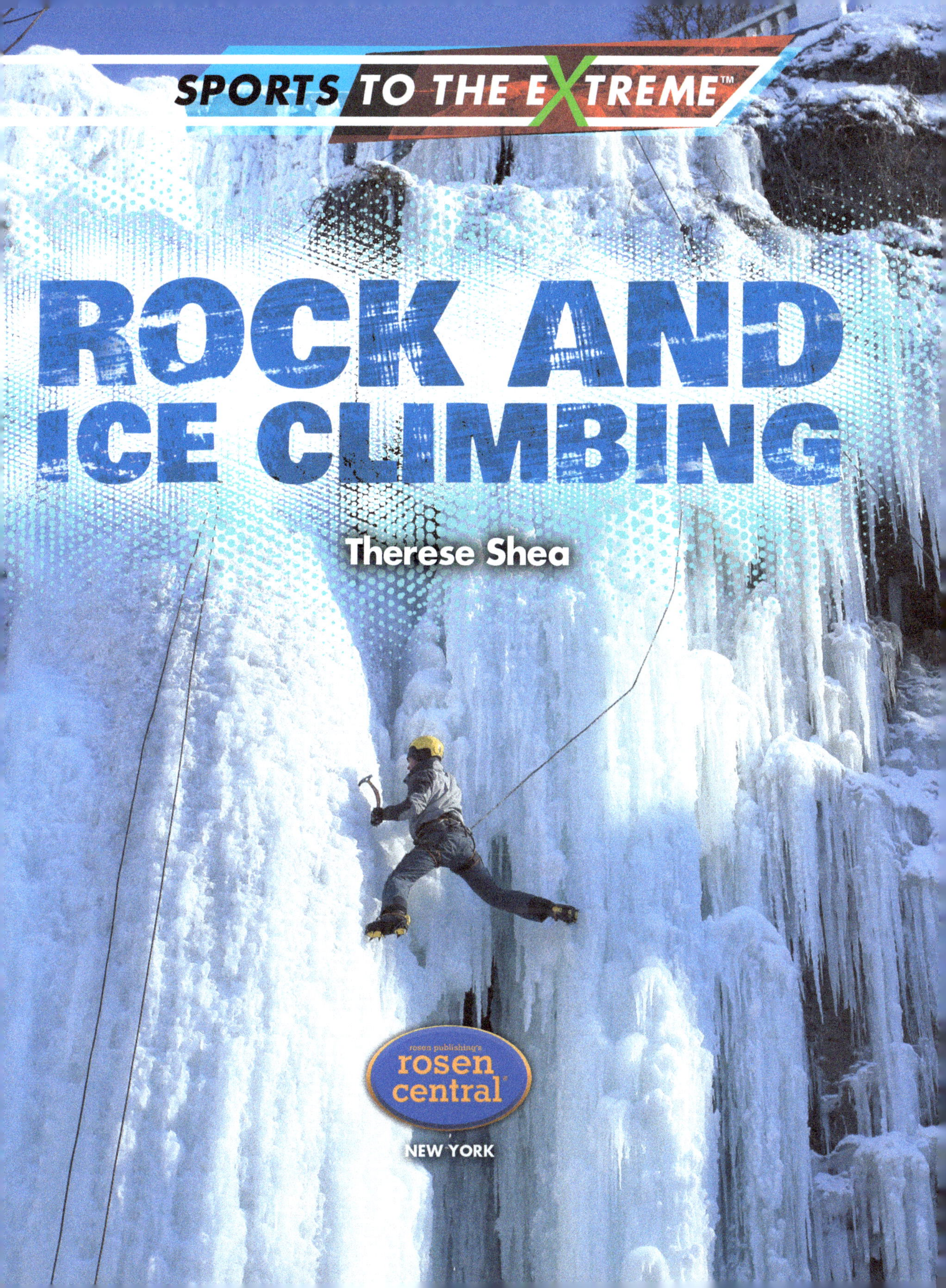

rosen publishing's rosen central®

NEW YORK

Published in 2016 by The Rosen Publishing Group, Inc.
29 East 21st Street, New York, NY 10010

First Edition

Library of Congress Cataloging-in-Publication Data

Shea, Therese.
Rock and ice climbing/Therese Shea.—First Edition.
pages cm.—((Sports to the Extreme))
Includes bibliographical references and index.
Audience: Grades: 5–8.
ISBN 978-1-4994-3557-3 (Library bound) — ISBN 978-1-4994-3559-7 (Paperback) —
ISBN 978-1-4994-3560-3 (6-pack)
1. Rock climbing—Juvenile literature. 2. Snow and ice climbing—Juvenile literature. I. Title.
GV200.2.S475 2015
796.522'3—dc23

2014041528

Manufactured in the United States of America